Creepers and Copers

Ranking Your Male Admirers for Safety, Fun and (Maybe) Friendship

John Combest

St. Louis, Missouri, USA

Copyright © 2025 Read the Comments, LLC, Missouri

Chapters and case studies employ fictitious characters and events to illustrate the process of assessing and managing male admirers. Any resemblance to actual persons, living or dead, or actual events is purely coincidental.

This book is not intended to diagnose or treat any physical or mental illness or injury. The information offered is not medical or psychiatric advice and does not replace the need for medical and/or mental health care. We are certainly not curing cancer here.

All brand names and trademarks mentioned herein are the property of their respective owners.

References to brand names are for fictional storytelling purposes only. Nothing in the body of the text, appendix or case studies should be construed as financial, legal, tax, or investment advice.

No part of this book may be reproduced, or stored in a retrieval system, or transmitted in any form or by any means, electronic, mechanical, photocopying, recording, or otherwise, without express written permission of the publisher.

Library of Congress Control Number: 2025902768

ISBN-13: 979-8-9873389-3-3

Printed in the United States of America

For the LLC

Contents

Chapter 1: Not a dating book 1

Chapter 2: The Global Thirst Marketplace 2

Chapter 3: Morality disclaimer 6

Chapter 4: Mental models 7

Chapter 5: Ego and narcissism 9

Chapter 6: Pedestalization 11

Chapter 7: White Knight Syndrome 13

Chapter 8: Covert contracts 15

Chapter 9: Cope 18

Chapter 10: Male Admirer Matrix 20

Chapter 11: Moth Men 24

Chapter 12: Creepers 29

Chapter 13: Stepstools 34

Chapter 14: Copers 39

Chapter 15: The Unicorn 44

Epilogue: The MAGA Myth 53

Appendix: Findom 56

Book club discussion #1: The Moth Man Surplus 57

Book club discussion #2: The Smarmy Stepstool 62

Gratitude 66

Chapter 1: Not a dating book

This is not a dating book. The male admirers referenced in this book are not the men for whom you have a genuine, burning desire.[1] In the following chapters, you'll recognize archetypes of men in your life:

- ➢ Long-suffering "nice guys" with a crush
- ➢ Social media stalkers
- ➢ Creepy customers and/or clients
- ➢ Ex-boyfriends
- ➢ "Work husbands"

Even the random men on the fringe of your social circle from whom you receive the slack-jawed awestruck male gaze.

On your most visceral (read: authentic) level, you've already deemed these men unworthy of your physical intimacy. The men we're scrutinizing and assessing in this book don't deserve romantic relationship status with you. If this is causing a moral dilemma, we'll address it in Chapter 3.

---

[1] Richard Cooper, The Unplugged Alpha (Whitby, Ontario: Richard Cooper, 2020), 42.

Chapter 2: The Global Thirst Marketplace

"(S)ocial media is not universally destroying youths' self-esteem ... Twenty years ago, an 18-year-old in (America) received superficial external validation primarily from men (or women) in their hometown. Today, posting a flattering swimsuit picture of themselves on Instagram can score thousands of 'likes' from low-value simps around the world."[2]

For all the benefits of social media, it's never been harder to assess and rank your male admirers.

When Generation X and elder millennials were in their teens and twenties, men's seduction strategies were in plain sight:

- ➢ The "nice guy" who acted like he wanted to be friends but criticized every man his crush dated.
- ➢ The guy on the fringe of the social circle calling a girl's home phone (a landline!) asking her to hang out.

---

[2] John Combest. "20 for 20, Part 2." The Missouri Times, October 19, 2021

➤ The manager at the retail store assigning better hours and longer smoke breaks to the employees that went out drinking with him after work.

In marketing terms, women on social media today have an exponentially wider top of the funnel than women did decades ago. But without in-person social cues, it's harder to judge each man entering that funnel. Is he well-groomed or smelly? Confident in his own skin, or just posturing? Is he *really* 6 feet tall?

Men, being men, take every advantage of online subterfuge. Witness the masculinity coaches who promise to improve dating app profiles with lighting tricks, status flexing and outdoor animal pics. Who wouldn't swipe right, their theory goes, on a man posing with a horse?

With a glut in the worldwide supply of thirsty men, face-to-face screening isn't always an option. A fast and reliable mental model helps categorize male admirers quickly.

Female wisdom in the workplace: A generation denied

Ask a woman who worked in a corporate environment as recently as the early 2010s and they'll confirm knowledge and information about male coworkers was passed about freely. There's a good chance the wisdom flowed from a middle-aged woman who called herself a "salty broad" and seemed to know a little *too* much about executives' personal lives.

Paradoxically, the ascent of women in the modern workplace – and the evolution of sexual harassment and equal opportunity protections - has made identification of creepers and "nice guys" more difficult.

The very policies and guidelines that protect women from unwanted advances restrict office "gossip" and hostile work environments. In practical terms the policies that keep a creeper from accosting female coworkers can keep those same female coworkers from thwarting him.

The vigilance against workplace sexual harassment and intimidation – and the actions backing up those policies – are critical to working toward greater opportunity and achievement. <u>They are a net positive development for women.</u>

But they also limit the knowledge that, in a bygone era, was passed from experienced women to new female employees.

The result is a modern generation of women professionals often deprived and denied the benefit of collective female wisdom and experience. This book in some ways can recreate that structure through a useful mental model and relatable archetypes.

But first, on to Chapter 3 – where we'll check the angel on your shoulder.

Chapter 3: Morality disclaimer

"If the world is like a giant scheming court and we are trapped inside it, there is no use in trying to opt out of the game. That will only render you powerless, and powerlessness will make you miserable." – Robert Greene, The 48 Laws of Power

This book is about what works and not about what is right and wrong.

"Power is essentially amoral and one of the most important skills to acquire is the ability to see circumstances rather than good or evil. Power is a game — this cannot be repeated too often — and in games you do not judge your opponents by their intentions but by the effect of their actions."[3]

If you choose to view intersexual dynamics through a binary right versus wrong or good versus evil standard, you should stop reading now. You'll miss out on the fun, but can preserve your moral superiority.

---

[3] Robert Greene, The 48 Laws of Power (London: Profile Books, 2010), page xix

Chapter 4: Mental models

A mental model is a shorthand way to save time, a heuristic.

You are already sizing up the men you encounter in person and online. Using a clear, dual-axis mental model will help you organize your assessments in a more consistent way and allow the identification of common characteristics to further save you time.

Rian Stone writes: "Purposeful, useful created narratives are called mental models... You may already have some... When you are indoctrinated into (Christianity) you are provided mental models which anchor your decisions to that identity. The heuristic, 'What would Jesus do?' is an example."[4]

As Stone notes, mental models are meant to be taken seriously - not literally - and you can expect other people to nitpick aspects of your mental model.

"No one else has to believe or endorse your models, and other people having different mental models

---

[4] Rian Stone, Frame (Canada: Rian Stone, 2022), First Edition

doesn't invalidate them for you. They are all simply tools in a box."[5]

Before diving into the mental model, it's essential to explore the top driver of a man's conscious behavior: his ego.

---

[5] Ibid.

Chapter 5: Ego and narcissism

"Narcissism is the male condition." – Rian Stone, Frame

Who among us hasn't had a friend that described the reason for her breakup as, "He was a total narcissist!"

The Diagnostic and Statistical Manual of Mental Disorders (DSM) has a practicing psychology definition of narcissistic personality disorder (NPD), but for our purposes, we'll turn to Stone to define the common trait in men.

Stone writes that a narcissist creates "an identity (in other words, he makes one up) and requires everyone around him to reinforce it."

Multiple definitions of narcissism exist in pop culture, but there's one fundamental truth to understand your male admirers' behavior:

The male ego must be protected at all costs.

Acknowledging that narcissism is the male condition – *even among the "nice guys" and "work husbands" you know* – can make it easier to identify a man's go-to form of ego protection. Each of your admirers has one.

In the next 4 chapters, we'll describe four common ego defense mechanisms (EDMs) as they manifest in the four types of male admirers. You'll spot familiar patterns from the men in your life, gain a deeper understanding of defensive behaviors, and see how each directly affects admirers' behavior toward you.

Chapter 6: Pedestalization

"Submissive, accommodating, neurotic and pandering are all cooperative lower status behaviors. Signaling and acceptance of one's lower status is driven by a need to impress or pander to those they consider above them." - Rian Stone, Frame

Status imbalance is the cornerstone of **pedestalization**. Status is contextual and can be related to physical attractiveness, social standing, "clout," workplace/career status, or some combination thereof.

The male ego must be protected at all costs.

Pedestalization protects the male ego by avoiding direction rejection. It's a form of self-disqualification; a man signals he lacks the status to make a serious play for your affections, and therefore "isn't even trying." And if he's not really trying, his ego remains unthreatened.

Good boy points and pats on the head

Along with cope (Chapter 9), pedestalization is a socially acceptable form of expressing adoration and desire. It's widely considered non-threatening and has the added benefit of earning the admirer platonic praise for his "good boy" behavior.

12

Being put on a pedestal can be flattering, but what's with the men who think you need to be saved? Read on.

Chapter 7: White Knight Syndrome

Men with **White Knight Syndrome** feel an overwhelming delusional burden of knowing what's best for a woman while being unable to force her to act accordingly.

White Knight Syndrome can be summarized by two ego-fueled mantras:

> ➢ "If she knew what I knew, she would choose me."
> ➢ "I can save her."

Men with White Knight Syndrome diagnose a woman's particular situation and portray it as a predicament only he can solve. He's a mechanic with X-ray vision; he need not actually look under the hood to know exactly how the engine operates. And he's the only trained professional in town with the expertise and equipment to give the woman a proper tune-up.

White Knights are resistant to – and sometimes incapable of - processing and accepting rejection, whether indirect or direct.

The male ego must be protected at all costs.

The only reason you've not yet fallen in love with the White Knight, he reasons, is that you simply don't understand how perfect he is.

White Knight Syndrome in men leads to behaviors that women recognize as pushy, needy, and manipulative. White Knight Syndrome demands validation more desperately than other ego defense mechanisms and most closely fits the Stone definition of narcissism (Chapter 5) – its self-insistent wisdom and brilliance must be acknowledged, *or else.*

Chapter 8: Covert contracts

A covert contract is any arrangement in which you believe another person or group of people is obligated to behave toward you in a certain way, and the other party is unaware that the obligation exists. In other words, the "contract" exists only in your head.[6]

Day after day, you've encountered men's **covert contracts** – you just haven't yet had a precise term to label the ick.

At a bar, a guy buys drinks for you and your friends – and expects you to talk to him at least until the "free" drink is empty.

In college, a male classmate or teacher's assistant offers study materials or valuable tutoring – then expects study-buddy sessions to be a regular occurrence.

In the workplace, a higher-level male colleague offers advice and mentoring – away from the office,

---

[6] John Combest, Stalking, Harassment, Internet Trolling: A Guide to Recovering and Rebuilding After Online Attacks (St. Louis, Missouri: John Combest, 2022), p. 89

first over coffee or lunch and eventually at dinner and drinks.

You might not have heard the term "covert contracts" until now, but the strings-attached feeling is all too familiar.

"The overwhelming majority of covert contracts are ultimately unfulfilled. Why? We can't expect someone to uphold their end of a bargain if they don't even know the obligation exists."[7]

Rollo Tomassi coined "The Martyr Schema" and "The Friends Debt" to describe two understated seduction gambits used by self-described "nice guys."[8] Self-sacrifice and pseudo-friendship, Tomassi notes, are used as cover to mask desire and avoid direct rejection.

The male ego must be protected at all costs.

Observe the unspoken

You are not responsible for correcting, calling out or canceling a man's covert contracts. Male admirers employing covert contracts take steps toward an imaginary finish line they'll never reach – a fantasy-fueled pot of gold at the end of your rainbow.

---

[7] Combest, ibid.
[8] Rollo Tomassi, The Rational Male (Nevada: Counterflow Media LLC, 2013), 64.

The frustration and angst caused by covert contracts are particularly evident among men in Chapters 12 and 13. One group is prone to lashing out, and another group may make unwelcome/uninvited advances based on the quid pro quo that exists in their head.

But what about the men who insist they don't want anything from you? *Sure*, they admit, they *might have a little crush* on you but swear they can keep their desires in check. These men have their own method of ego protection called cope.

Chapter 9: Cope

Once considered strictly a verb, **"cope"** has rightfully evolved into a noun – and this ego-protection strategy is a staple in the mental diet of modern men.

You overhear cope from men every day. *Everywhere.*

At the gym, around his gym bros: "I could have played <insert sport> in college, but I got hurt."

In the workplace, around his peers: "I should have been promoted a long time ago, but the boss is an idiot. I wouldn't want that management job anyway!"

<u>For our purposes, cope is any rationalization a man makes for why he's not in a physically intimate relationship with a woman he desires.</u>

Cope can range from reasonable and factual (e.g., "She has a boyfriend," "I'm her boss") to delusional and speculative (e.g., "If she had met me before she met her boyfriend, we'd be together now.")

When the discomfort of current reality (i.e., lacking an intimate relationship with you) is too much for a man to bear, he injects cope-ium straight into his veins.

"She's just working on herself right now and isn't in the right headspace for a relationship." Cope.

"She really values our friendship and doesn't want to risk losing that." Cope.

"I kind of look like her boyfriend. If she had met me first, she would have been all over me!" Cope.

The male ego must be protected at all costs.

As we'll explore in Chapter 14, Cope-ium addiction isn't limited to derelicts or broken men. On the contrary, almost every viable candidate for your friendship employs cope.

Now that we've identified the top methods of male ego protection, it's time to evaluate your admirers' behavior on two key scales: Intrusiveness and Utility.

Chapter 10: Male Admirer Matrix

The core mental model of this book is the Male Admirer Matrix. Once the concept of the two axes is established in your mind, you can quickly and reliably place current and future male admirers into their proper category and reassess as circumstances change.

On the vertical (Y) axis is intrusiveness (unintrusive to intrusive.) On the horizontal (X) axis is utility (useless to useful.)

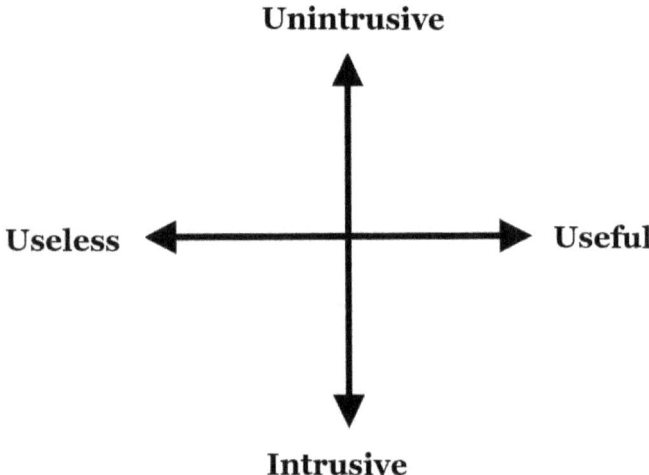

Intrusiveness (Y axis)

On this axis we judge the individual male's intrusiveness. This is a relative measurement of "creepiness" or "ick"; to be more precise, assess the behaviors that demonstrate *uninvited* encroachment into your physical space, personal and/or professional life, social media orbit, or combination thereof.

In person:

> - Uninvited lingering gazes (staring)
> - Attempts to manufacture and maintain eye contact
> - Attempts to manufacture physical proximity
> - Attempts to manufacture "random" commonalities
> - Attempts to get "caught" talking about you to others
> - Attempts to manufacture friendships with your family, male friends and romantic interests

Social media

> - Watching your TikToks, Snaps, Instagram and Facebook stories
> - Mining your social posts to manufacture "random" commonalities and interests

- Following your friends, acquaintances, co-workers and family members
- Watching your friends' and family's TikToks, Snaps, Instagram and Facebook stories

Professional/career

- Showing up at your workplace more than normal or necessary (customers)
- Lingering at workplace after hours (customers in service industry)
- Scheduling himself to work overlapping shifts with you (co-workers)
- Inserting himself into your workstreams to force interaction (co-workers)
- Seeking control via management or oversight/approval on your projects (co-workers/managers)

Utility (X axis)

On this axis we assess the male admirer's relative usefulness. We're assessing his usefulness *at this moment*, not necessarily at some undefined moment in the future. For example, a male admirer currently in law school is of less utility than a full-fledged attorney partner at a law firm.

Tangible utility

- Monetary tips or commissions (service industry)

- Gifts
- Meals/drinks
- Tickets (concerts, exclusive parties, sports)
- Amazon wishlists ("Spoil me" links to clothing, tech)
- OnlyFans/Fansly/Patreon subscription fees
- Bill payments
- Trips (airfare, meals, spa treatments, entertainment)

Intangible utility

- Access to professional connections (job interviews, letters of recommendations, introductions)
- Social proof (e.g., an influencer who could get you more customers and/or more followers on social)
- Foil (evoke competition anxiety in boyfriend/romantic interest; evoke envy in female acquaintances and frienemies)
- Emotional tampon (shoulder to cry on, reliable and instant validation)
- Errand boy (on-call sober driver, apartment/house handyman, lawn service provider)

Now that we have two criteria by which to judge, it's time to build out the mental model and put your male admirers in their proper places.

Chapter 11: Moth Men

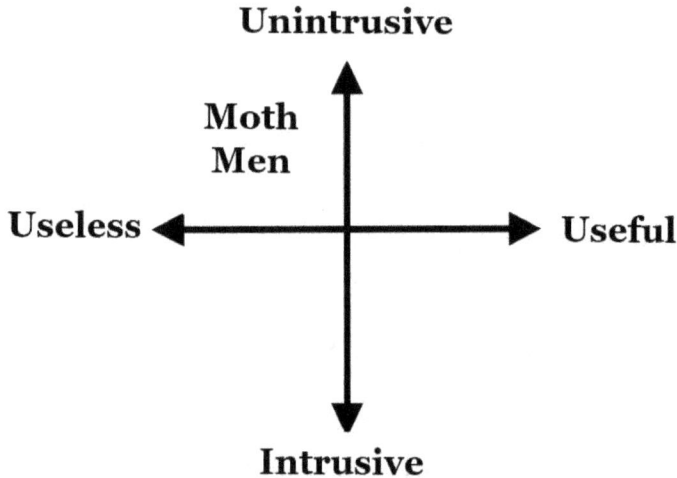

Quadrant profile: Unintrusive, useless

Like moths to a flame, your male admirers are initially attracted by your heat and light. A group of literal moths is called an eclipse, but a group of Moth Men can magnify – rather than block – your image to the world.

Moth Men are easy to spot in the wild. In virtual spaces, you'll find them in your comments and replies, replying with heart-eye emojis on your pics and videos. In person, they're likely to stare intently to get your attention, then immediately break eye contact if you look their way.

A Moth Man's primary Ego Defense Mechanism is pedestalization. Moth Men know their role and are careful not to overstep boundaries by asking personal questions or seeking to engage in anything beyond superficial low-risk conversations. It's unclear – and irrelevant – whether their intentional distance is due to low self-esteem and fear of rejection, or general low effort.

Benefits: Moth Men are not *entirely* useless; a swarm of Moth Men can boost engagement metrics on social platforms and can help pad the numbers for social proof. Women who have little interest in social media metrics will find Moth Men to be of zero collective significance.

Moth Men are often the most plentiful men in your orbit because their incremental investment is low – usually only costing them brief moments of their time. They are a mere commodity, a unit of inventory in your life, and the global supply of Moth Men will generally outpace your demand.

Moth Men are the only category of males within the Male Admirer Matrix that willingly accept asymmetrical desire – a concept we'll explore in Chapter 16.

Risks: Being too charitable with your interactions (e.g., giving their Instagram comment a heart-on) can embolden Moth Men to become more intrusive and move into Creeper territory (Chapter 12.)

Best case: Lateral movement across the X (Usefulness) axis and no movement down the Y (Intrusiveness) axis. Since Moth Men are risk-averse, the optimal way to nudge them along the usefulness axis is by appealing to their pedestalization cravings.

Moth Men can scratch their pedestalization itch by:
- Buying from your Amazon, SHEIN and other wish lists (see Appendix: Findom)
- Paying monthly tribute through Premium Snapchat, OnlyFans, Fansly, Patreon and other subscription services
- Subsidizing multilevel marketing (MLM) sales programs
- Tipping/overtipping (service industry)

Worst case: Moth Men may move down the Intrusiveness scale and become Creepers. At times, the transition to Creeper is out of your control.

In virtual environments, a Moth Man's compulsive viewing of your posts may create a false sense of intimacy and insight into your wants and needs. <u>Men are virtually unable to possess knowledge and opinions without sharing, especially if they feel flexing the knowledge will impress others.</u>

In real-world face-to-face environments, repeated physical proximity makes it more likely he'll "bump into" you and force you to engage in polite interaction. His rehearsed pitch and canned lines are dead giveaways to the preparation put into the not-at-all spontaneous moment, and proof he has metamorphosized from Moth Man to Creeper.

You can't control a Moth Man's flight to your flame, so focus on what you *can* control. Treating a Moth Man as you'd treat a friend (e.g., liking their replies, responding to their questions) encourages further interaction and solidifies their false sense of intimacy. If you choose to engage with Moth Men, every interaction should be focused on moving them across the Utility axis, encouraging actions that directly and tangibly benefit you – without intruding on your time or emotional space.

Since their incremental time investments are relatively insignificant, Moth Men often cast a wide net to several women at a time. Expect to see churn in Moth Men, with some longtime admirers leaving your comment/reply sections in search of more responsive targets.

Moth Men are like compulsive slot machine players – they'll keep sliding their attention coins into the dark void as long as it gives them the illusion of a potential jackpot. In reality, the action is almost always fruitless self-soothing.

Chapter 12: Creepers

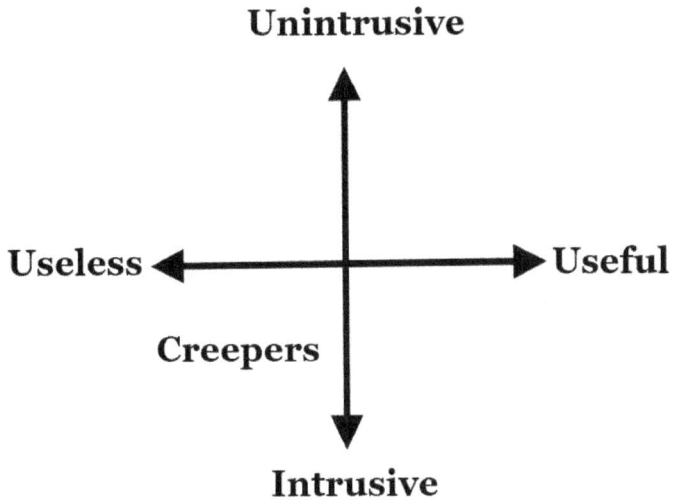

Quadrant profile: Intrusive, useless

Hovering. Staring. Pressing. Hounding. The Creeper never met an unspoken boundary he wouldn't violate or a subtle cue he understood.

A Creeper's primary Ego Defense Mechanism is White Knight Syndrome. The Creeper is the playwright of a heroic tale co-starring you as the damsel in distress. He casts himself as the leading man, destined to save you from your current unfortunate predicament. The hero's journey involves showing and telling you what you're missing, enlightening you until you have no choice but to be swept off your feet.

Likely a student of romantic comedies, the Creeper is convinced your lack of interest – or active *un*interest - is due to an unfortunate gap in your knowledge. He assigns himself the duty of educating you.

No number of facts or rejections will get in the way of his plot resolution. Any inconvenient truths – your clear signals of displeasure, the presence of a boyfriend or husband – are mere hurdles that he, the main character, must overcome in his chivalrous conquest.

Benefits: None. Creepers are universally a net negative value proposition. Any tiny incremental value they provide (e.g., boosting your social media follower count and/or engagement metrics) is wiped out by the stress, generalized ick and overall discomfort they bring into your world.

Risks: Creepers are the most volatile of the four admirer profiles; their intrusiveness usually involves some form of stalking, whether virtual or in real life.

Unfortunately, dissuading a Creeper isn't easy.

In the workplace, men whom you could ignore in other venues (e.g., avert their gaze on the street or distance yourself in a social situation) may be part of your everyday work environment. You are generally bound by professional courtesy in the workplace, and Creepers take the opportunity to force interactions.

Creepers struggle with the concept of sunk costs. In financial terms, a sunk cost is an allocation of resources for which the value will not be recovered (e.g., purchasing a derelict house in a neighborhood of declining property value.)

In a Creeper's mind, his emotional and time investment **must** be recovered. This is his highest priority. Like unsuccessful investors, Creepers are willing to pour more resources – namely time and energy – into an investment that is not paying off. This fuels an intense obsession with "winning" your affection.

Best case: Exiting your life, by virtue of becoming bored from lack of engagement or finding another target to creep on.

More likely, though, you'll need to employ one of four strategies:

    1.) <u>Direct rejection.</u> A polite, "I'm not interested," will in rare cases suffice. Engaging a Creeper with additional details or rationalizing *why* you're not interested can perpetuate his White Knighting. Attempting to prove his value and demonstrate what you're missing out on leads to a doom loop of effort and rejection for the Creeper.

2.) <u>Ghosting, blocking and grey rocking.</u> Removing your physical presence is sometimes an option in real-life face-to-face situations. Blocking his accounts from viewing your posts and stories can be done on nearly every social media platform. And grey rocking – providing bare minimum factual statements with no emotional content – can work for situations where you're forced to interact.

3.) <u>Social pressure.</u> When a Creeper is part of your social circle, a man of equal or higher status in the group may be leveraged to dissuade intrusive behavior. This is most effective if the conversation is non-confrontational and doesn't encourage the Creeper to take a defiant oppositional stance. The male admirers in Chapter 14 are especially useful for the assignment.

4.) <u>Chain of command.</u> In the workplace, inform your manager that the Creeper co-worker or customer is making you uncomfortable and affecting your ability to do your job. Outside of the workplace, consult stalking/harassment resources. In cases in which your safety or the safety of others is reasonably at risk, contact law enforcement.

Worst case: Increasing obsession (fixating on you) and compulsion (stalking behaviors) leading to threats to you and/or men in your life. Again: in cases in which your safety or the safety of others is reasonably at risk, contact law enforcement.

For practical purposes, Creepers are irredeemable. You might feel pangs of guilt for rejecting him so bluntly or second-guess whether you did something to lead him on. On the contrary – he either misread or ignored your cues early on. You are never obligated to play a co-starring role in any male admirer's romantic fantasy.

Chapter 13: Stepstools

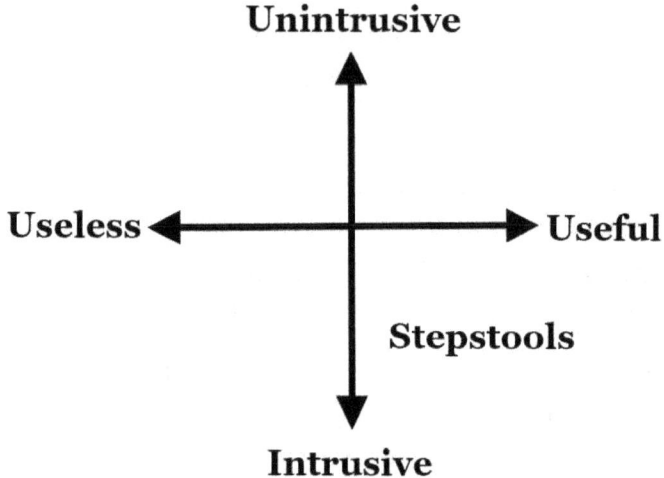

Quadrant profile: Intrusive, useful

You could reach them on your own, without help. The fine china in your upper kitchen cabinet, the cashmere sweater on your top closet shelf.

Your next financial objective, the next rung on the corporate ladder.

You could get up on your toes, stretch a bit and grab them for yourself.

But what if a stepstool was positioned strategically – sitting *right there* - for you to use whenever and wherever you wanted a little upward boost?

Human Stepstools are heavier and harder to move than the metal, plastic and wooden versions. And unlike the inanimate ones, human Stepstools are guaranteed to try to peek up your skirt. But chances are you have more of the latter at your disposal than the ones you'd find in housewares.

A Stepstool's primary Ego Defense Mechanism is Covert Contracts. The Stepstool believes he can't win your affection with his personality and/or looks alone – *for now*. He needs to offer you an incentive, he reasons, to get close to him. He shows off high-status cues (e.g., personal wealth, professional and social accomplishments) to signal the benefits of getting close to him.

Like drug dealers and credit card companies, Stepstools' initial offerings come with no immediate payment required and seemingly no strings attached. Over time, as favors become more significant, you're accumulating a debt on his mental balance sheet. And the preferred form of payment isn't thank-you texts or friendly hugs.

Benefits: Stepstools, as their name suggests, are useful tools to be stepped upon. In some cases, the man may have been born into his elevated status, or acquired resources (e.g., money, social status) through similar luck.

In many cases, though, Stepstools achieved their elevated status through some combination of technical skill and hard work. Instead of making them more humble, the climb up the financial/career/social ladder has made them cocky. The fruits of their upward climb include not just monetary reward, they reason, but greater access to desirable women in need.

Stepstools provide tangible and intangible boosts.

Tangible benefits can include monetary tips, meals and drinks, commissions (via donations and contributions) for salespeople and professional fundraisers, concert tickets and VIP passes, airline tickets and hotel rooms, and gifts purchased from online retailer wish lists.

Intangible benefits include job recommendations and leads, invitations to elite social and professional gatherings and informal networks, valuable career advice and mentoring – just to name a few.

Risks: Stepstools exhibit the same intrusive behavior profile as Creepers and carry the same risks. *Stepstools are Creepers with higher status and/or resources.* Remember this if you choose to engage with Stepstools in a professional/workplace environment.

Best case: A Stepstool is most useful if he fulfils the obligations of his own covert contract without reminding you of the debt you're accruing in his mind. In other words, make space for each Stepstool in your figurative closet as long as it's functional whenever you need it – on *your* terms.

Scenarios in which these male admirers provide long-term reliable utility:

- Some Stepstools ascend to a professional level in which the fear of losing their job outweighs the urge to cash in their intimacy chips with a co-worker or professional associate.
- Proximity changes (new job, relocation to another city) can make his push/pull for in-person meetings with you less frequent or nonexistent.
- Entering a new exclusive relationship could pause his pursuit.
- An influx of other viable targets could reduce the frequency and intensity of his intrusive behavior, while still keeping him on call when he can be of service to you.

Worst case: Some Stepstools collapse under the weight of their own covert contracts. If a Stepstool believes he's provided *too much* value and received an insufficient intimacy payoff from you, he may react in one of two ways:

1.) <u>Forcing the issue.</u> A Stepstool may choose to cash in his chips with an aggressive push – an in-person physical advance or a verbal/text ultimatum.
2.) <u>Passive-aggressive sulking/butthurt.</u> More likely than a direct confrontation, a Stepstool may turn to obstinance. He may uncharacteristically ignore your texts, minimize or demean your requests for personal and professional help, all to get you to ask a subservient, "Have I done something wrong?"

Your interests, his resources, on your terms

Some of them want to use you

Some of them want to get used by you

Some of them want to abuse you

Some of them want to be abused – Eurythmics[9]

A Stepstool places himself at your feet – offering to lift you up in the unspoken hope that one day he can get on top. A reminder from Chapter 8 - you are not responsible for correcting, calling out or canceling a man's covert contracts. Step on him to get what you want, when you want it, on your terms.

---

[9] "Sweet Dreams (Are Made of This)," Eurythmics, Sweet Dreams (Are Made of This), RCA, 1983, Track 6

Chapter 14: Copers

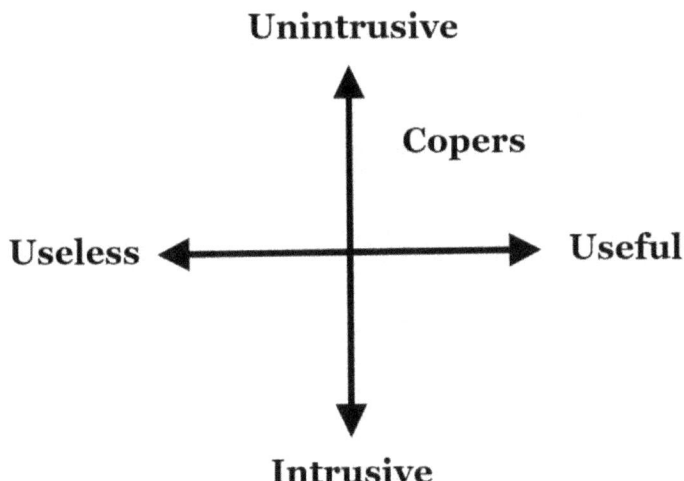

Quadrant profile: Unintrusive, useful

As you walk the crowded street along the Boulevard of Broken Men[10], you swat away the swarms of Moth Men and avoid eye contact with the Creepers. You smirk walking past the high-end restaurants your Stepstools invite you to for "mentoring sessions" until you see the quiet bar at the northeast corner of Unintrusive and Useful.

---

[10] "Boulevard of Broken Dreams," Green Day, American Idiot, Reprise, 2004, Track 4

As you step inside and adjust to the soft warm light, you saunter toward a crew of your favorite male admirers. They've saved you a seat and have already ordered your signature drink.

These are your friends. These are your Copers.

A Coper's primary Ego Defense Mechanism is cope. Copers love telling their meet-cute story of how they first made your acquaintance, and they can recite every detail of the initial encounter. (You may or may not even remember the occasion.) They're also quick with a follow-up narrative around why exactly the two of you aren't a couple.

Copers include:

- "Work husbands"
- Ex-lovers who didn't go psycho
- Guys you friendzoned early and who took it like a champ.

Benefits: Copers can serve the same function as your favorite girlfriends. While your Copers might not see things from a female perspective, you get the benefit of a male perspective on your personal and professional challenges.

Risks: Copers are comfortable acknowledging your shared emotional intimacy, but they rarely acknowledge their physical attraction to you. Two main reasons:

1.) <u>"Not like other guys" syndrome.</u> Many Copers want you to consider them a "good guy" and think hiding their attraction will elevate them above common lustful men in your eyes.

2.) <u>Unaddressed desire.</u> In many cases, Copers have internalized shame about their visceral attraction to you and can't admit it to themselves. And if they can't admit it to themselves, they certainly won't confess it to you. After all, what if you tell them you're *still* not as attracted to them as they are to you?

The male ego must be protected at all costs.

Your physical presence involuntarily revs your male admirers' engines, and Copers are the only group in the Male Admirer Matrix that slam their feet on the brake. The ensuing cognitive dissonance – an overwhelming desire for you, while simultaneously experiencing no physical or emotional release – is too much for many Copers to bear over the long term. As the weight of their frustration builds, Copers may devolve into intrusive behavior.

Best case: A Coper embodies a (paraphrased) maxim of Rollo Tomassi: "If you're not her boyfriend, you're her girlfriend."[11] Copers burrow deeply into their cozy rationalizations for why the two of you *could* be together but *choose* not to be - as if he has any say in the matter.

Nestled safely in his den of delusion, a Coper may demonstrate in word and deed the actions of a loyal friend. Lifelong, rewarding friendships are possible so long as the coping cocoon is undisturbed.

Worst case: By the time a man enters your Coper cadre, you've already pre-selected him as someone who doesn't give you the ick (i.e., he has low intrusiveness) and who provides significant value to your life. But that doesn't mean things can't go south.

For some Copers, the aforementioned cognitive dissonance of *desiring you* yet *not having you* is too much to bear. There are countless ways he could act out - a chemical-induced confessional proclaiming his love for you, a text message dissertation about how your boyfriend/husband is *so* not right for you, even petulant in-person mocking and undermining of your current romantic partner or prospects.

The uninvited meddling in your romantic relationship(s) moves him down the Y axis (Intrusiveness). At the same time, he's proving to be

---

[11] Rollo Tomassi, The Rational Male (Nevada: Counterflow Media LLC, 2013), 76-78

less valuable as a trusted friend - moving him to the left on the X axis (Utility.)

Suddenly, you've lost a Coper and gained a Creeper.

Copers offer the usefulness of Stepstools with the reliable adoration of Moth Men. But there's still the lingering unspoken attraction, the tension.

In the category of male admirers, can anything beat a Coper? Yes.

Chapter 15: The Unicorn

In the last chapter we saw the value of Copers. They're the only category of men within the Male Admirer Matrix suitable to be your friend.

But what if there was a category of men *even better* suited to be your friend than Copers?

Enter the Unicorn.

Unicorns earn their classification by being nearly impossible to find in the wild. Some believe they don't exist at all. By the end of this chapter, you might be convinced that if Unicorns are in fact real, they must be *made* and not *born*.

Since they may or not be real, we'll place Unicorns outside the Male Admirer Matrix universe.

Like Copers, Unicorns rank high on usefulness and low on intrusiveness. Unlike Copers, Unicorns have consciously chosen to shed self-delusions. *Unicorns are Copers without the cope.*

Why is it important to distinguish between Unicorns and Copers?

Many – if not most - Copers operate under a covert contract *with themselves* – the notion that one day, if the circumstances are just right – he might have a shot at you. Unicorns, on the other hand, have shed covert contracts with themselves and **accept your relationship as it is in this moment.**

The Unicorn Checklist

"Scientists have developed a classification scheme that categorizes all members of the animal kingdom ... Animals have been traditionally classified according to two characteristics: body plan and developmental pathway." – Biology 2e, OpenStax[12]

We'll follow the model of the biological classification system to identify a Unicorn.

Body plan traits, related to the man himself and not directly involving you:

1.) **Abundance of options:** A Unicorn is either in a relationship with a woman he desires, and/or has multiple desirable women as options. This minimizes - though doesn't eliminate - the potential for developing ONEitis for you.[13]

2.) **Self-validation:** Unicorns engage in little to no approval-seeking behaviors. You won't

---

[12] Biology 2e by OpenStax: Chapter 27.2, "Features Used to Classify Animals"; full text at https://openstax.org/details/books/biology-2e
[13] "ONEitis: An unhealthy romantic obsession with a single person." Rollo Tomassi, The Rational Male (Nevada: Counterflow Media LLC, 2013), 3

see or hear a Unicorn boasting about romantic conquests, flexing status symbols, or congratulating their own career success on social media.

Copers, on the other hand, subtly seek external validation from women. For example, they may apply the romantic comedy advice, "To impress a woman, show her how great of a boyfriend you are to someone else." Copers ostentatiously display how sweet and thoughtful they are to their girlfriend or wife – when those chivalrous deeds are really about making themselves feel good.[14]

3.) **Inviolable trust:** Unicorns reveal no details of the emotional intimacy they share with female friends. They wouldn't *dare* betray confidential conversations, emotional face-to-face moments or highly charged private messages. Press them about those friends, and you'll get nothing more than an acknowledgment of the friendship and perhaps an endorsement of the friend's character and intelligence.

---

[14] Liz Plank, For the Love of Men (New York: St. Martin's Griffin, 2019), 104-05

Copers, on the other hand, may hint or outright brag about their emotional intimacy with female friends. Press them, and they may even position themselves as the prize and the friend as the pursuer. A Coper thinks this is a flex; rather, it signals his own glaring need for others' validation and approval.

Development pathway traits, related to how the man behaves and interacts with you:

4.) **No shame.** A Unicorn acknowledges his physical and emotional attraction to you. Whether unsolicited or through your playful prodding, having a man express his emotional attraction *now* preempts grand gestures and/or declarations of love *later*.

On the other hand, many – if not most - Copers find it hard to shed their self-imposed shame of physical attraction. In some cases, it's because a Coper does not want to be lumped in with the common Moth Men he sees staring at you in person and fawning over your social media posts. Like a beach ball held underwater, eventually a Coper's physical desire will pop up and blast him in the face.

5.) **Acceptance of asymmetrical desire.** A Unicorn understands his desire for you is stronger and more intense than your desire for him. He realizes that only a tiny percentage of the female population will develop a genuine burning desire[15] for him, and he doesn't resent you for not being in that small slice of the pie.

A Coper, however, finds asymmetrical desire an affront to his ego. He fixes this imbalance with a heaping helping of cope.

6.) **Acceptance of asymmetrical expression.** A Unicorn's attraction to you is not conditional upon you expressing attraction, affection or approval of him. He gives honest, insightful and meaningful compliments with no expectation for you to reciprocate. No dramatic pauses, no, "So, how do you feel about me?"

Copers, on the other hand, need occasional reassurance that they're an important person in your life. You may get the sense that he's fishing for compliments, and when that need

---

[15] Richard Cooper, The Unplugged Alpha (Whitby, Ontario: Richard Cooper, 2020), 42.

is not satiated, he may withdraw his attention to punish you.

7.) Know boundaries, no butthurt. Copers and Unicorns both demonstrate the social intelligence to identify boundaries you've set for physical and emotional intimacy. Though generally categorized by their non-intrusive behavior, both types of male admirers are likely to test your intimacy boundaries through physical, verbal or written (text) means.

"Boundaries get crossed ... the friendship either recovers, or it doesn't." – Anon.

The differentiator between Copers and Unicorns, then, is how each reacts to you enforcing boundaries.

Copers are most likely to get butthurt – either actively (e.g., lashing out verbally) or passive-aggressively (withdrawing, acting insolent or sullen.) They're already struggling to cope with asymmetrical desire (#5) and asymmetrical expression (#6), and testing boundaries is a failsafe way to get your immediate attention.

If and when Unicorns butt up against your boundaries and get put in check, they accept the rebuff without insolence or petulance.

8.) No mate guarding. Copers may occasionally show flashes of envy about other men – particularly new males entering your orbit. Unicorns, on the other hand, have no jealousy about your other male friends, flings, boyfriends, and random romantic prospects. No, "That guy's not good enough for you." *Envy and competition anxiety are markings of a Coper, not a Unicorn.*

9.) No faux bro flexing. Copers may attempt to befriend your boyfriend, husband, or guys you're dating. Whether or not this is subconscious cuckoldry depends upon the individual male.

Beyond in-person social pleasantries, a Unicorn makes no attempt to ingratiate himself with your romantic interest(s) or social circle male friends. A Unicorn invariably has his own set of male friends and is not desperately seeking faux bros.

Faux bro creeping shows lack of respect for your healthy boundaries. "I'm friends with her boyfriend," is sneaking down the intrusive scale into Stepstool or even worse, Creeper.

10.) **Passes continual testing.** A Unicorn is not grandfathered into his status. He must continually prove his worthiness of your all-access friendship/security clearance.

Role of a Unicorn

Unicorns are the only category of male admirers that can be trusted with an all-access emotional intimacy pass.

A Unicorn serves all the useful roles of a Coper, but without your lingering self-doubt about "leading him on."

Actions that get a Unicorn demoted to Coper:

- Butthurt (pouting about boundaries, insolence and jealousy about new men entering your orbit)
- Forward-looking statements ("Maybe one day you'll …" statements suggesting the presence of a covert contract)
- Breaking the trust of your intimacy (sharing private information, pictures or screenshots)

> Chemical-induced honesty (e.g., only acknowledging his attraction to you when he's under the influence of substances.)

Do Unicorns Exist?

For family photographers, "unicorn photo shoots" provide magical experiences. With a simple strap-on horn and a sparkly saddle, an ordinary horse is transformed into an object of wonderment for young children.

After the shoot, the photog removes the horn and HeartSparkle reverts to Bill or Billy or Mack or Buddy.[16]

Was the experience magical? Absolutely.

Was the unicorn just a horse in disguise? Maybe. Does it matter?

Enjoy the Unicorn experience while it lasts, and don't be surprised if a playful tug makes his horn pop off.

---

[16] "All I Wanna Do," Sheryl Crow, Tuesday Night Music Club, A&M, 1993, Track 9

Epilogue: The MAGA Myth

No, not *that* MAGA.

Let's talk about Male Admirers Going Away.

Though not yet emblazoned on red hats, this MAGA theme is found in hundreds of persuasive TikTok and YouTube videos and thousands of X threads.

The Male Admirers Going Away thesis posits that social media is causing men to "wake up" to circumstances in which crafty women are taking advantage of well-intentioned – if dunderheaded – men.

Content creators sounding the MAGA alarm seem to represent all gender ideology camps. As you'd expect, their solutions are conveniently available for purchase – online courses for men teaching self-confidence and/or dating-app tips, or online courses for women teaching how to navigate the explosion of "red pill" and "black pill" men.

Are male admirers going away?

Color me skeptical.

A percentage of men – particularly young men of the modern "lost boys" generation – are finding comfort, humor and solace in self-professed alpha male influencers. And any given one of those lost-boys-to-men *might* choose to embark on a journey of ruthless self-examination.

He *might* test his socially-conditioned notions about masculinity and manhood, replacing transparent chestpuffery and false bravado with action and congruency.

He *might* stop making excuses and start doing the work.

He *might* stop complaining about his woman's "nagging" and start following through on that list of things he said he was going to do.

He *might* start addressing long-buried personal traumas and face his fears.

He *might* stop hiding behind his ego and instead use it as a sparring partner, training himself to get stronger every day.

But he won't.

The male ego must be protected at all costs.

The hypothetical man above will wilt when the "alpha male" journey gets too hard.

Male Admirers Going Away is a myth. Pedestalization, White Knight Syndrome, covert contracts and cope are real. Moth Men, Creepers, Stepstools and Copers are forever.

Don't believe me? Just ask a Unicorn.

Appendix: Findom

The explosion of subscription-based fan services (e.g., Patreon, OnlyFans, Fansly) has raised awareness of a unique niche of male-female relationship called financial domination ("findom.") For the purposes of our discussion, a findom relationship is one in which a dominant female rules over a submissive male, who pays a "tribute" to the female. In most cases, the tributes include cash, luxury items like shoes and handbags, or other high-ticket items like plane trips, cruises and resort stays.

Some entrepreneurs use their experience in the findom niche to sell courses instructing other women how to relieve male submissives ("paypigs" or "simps") of their money.

Aside from ethical considerations, financial domination is wrought with legal and tax questions as well (e.g., are tributes actually "gifts" or are they payment for a unique service?)

As with any industry, courses may range from the useful – authored by experienced and successful operators - to flimsy, artificial intelligence (AI)-generated PDFs. Some companies offer "freemium"-style products – for example, the SEO Bounty podcast episode called, "How To Get More Simps" pairs with upselling of other services.

Consult a tax attorney and/or therapist before beginning any findom program.

Book club discussion #1: The Moth Man Surplus

Olivia packed up her laptop and dropped a quick, "Have a good weekend!" to the office admin on the way out the door. The other junior account managers at the commercial real estate office left hours ago to play golf and smoke cigars with the bosses, but Olivia passed on the patriarchal ritual. She had playlists to put together.

She'd have a couple hours at home before heading out for the radio station's Friday live remote. Having majored in broadcasting in college Olivia knew the music radio industry provided fewer full-time jobs every year. That's what made her real estate 9-to-5 job so perfect – the salary and benefits provided the stability that part-time DJing never could. Olivia considered mixing tracks her art, and her weekend DJ gigs gave her a platform.

Olivia was used to male attention, but she was surprised by the sheer volume of men who hit on her at her first radio station events and bar/club gigs. She surmised a major factor was the swagger of the city's finance bros and the audacity of their new money. And of course the alcohol and edibles.

She was flattered by the comments she got every Friday on her "Liv Live" Instagram streams, the station's YouTube and Facebook streams and her own TikTok posts. She wasn't interested in using her platforms to find a boyfriend, *per se*, but she did see the social media engagement as an untapped and underutilized asset. It's a shame you can't deposit thirsty men into your bank account, she thought. Or *could* she?

One night Olivia heard a club bartender give a customer her Instagram name instead of a phone number. Olivia had an epiphany - what if she used her Instagram account as the top of a marketing funnel? Thanks to her day job, Olivia knew all about warm leads and conversion rates. But besides music mixes, what exactly was Olivia selling?

She opened her Instagram app on the spot and added her Amazon wish list to her profile. That's enough for now, she thought. She'd think this through when she got home.

Club regulars. Wannabe entertainers. Party promoters.

Olivia was building the list in her phone's Notes app. It was easy to tick through the types of men whose attention she captured.

The guys at real estate conferences hitting me up. The corporate bigshots in my LinkedIn inbox wanting to "connect." Every one of the "ur gorgeous!" guys in the station livestreams.

Olivia added her CashApp and Venmo accounts to her social profiles and created a LinkTree to centralize everything.

At live remotes, Olivia began taking requests through her Instagram as well as the station's request line. Her follower count jumped.

At her gigs, she posted a sign with her CashApp and Venmo for tips. The virtual cashbox jingled.

Olivia was packing up her DJ equipment at the bar one night when she saw an Amazon notification. A radio station's superfan bought her a new pair of headphones from her Wish List.

"This is what dancers must feel like when the last song ends and they pick up their tips from the stage," Olivia thought.

All the assets are ready.

The swimsuit photo shoot – *technically* the "radio station promo" shoot – produced amazing pics of Olivia at the turntables on a nearby beach. The station's marketing manager was all too pleased to use his personal high-def camera to shoot the shots.

The megamix audio files have been moved from SoundCloud to Olivia's hard drive and cloud account. She already has a new name for her music archive: "Re-Liv the Moment."

Only one question remained: OnlyFans or Patreon? Olivia mulled it over for weeks.

Subscription services give content creators the opportunity to convert their fans' loyalty and attention into monthly subscription income, and the upside potential seems significantly higher than typical female influencer profit models like recommending clothing and skin care products.

Olivia's best girlfriend at the real estate company – who works in human resources – suggested Patreon because of OnlyFans's stigma around "adult" content. But OnlyFans has its advantages too – and Olivia doesn't plan on posting adult content at all, just music mixes and some cute pics.

"So really, it's nothing more revealing than what I wear to the beach!" she argued in her head.

But the full-time gig is too good to risk with even the *perception* of naughtiness. Patreon it is.

Individual/book club discussion

1.) What are the most likely outcomes of Olivia attempting to convert her male admirers into paid subscribers?

2.) If you had a public-facing career or hobby like Olivia, would *you* create a subscriber-supported community?

3.) If Olivia asked you for advice before launching her Patreon, what would you tell her?

Book club discussion #2: The Smarmy Stepstool

"Where'th my hug?" the lispy manlet squeaked as he entered the ballroom.

The ick traveled straight from Robb's vocal cords into Maddie's ears and sent a flash of dryness through her body. She turned toward Robb and forced a smile, leaning down slightly to deliver an ass-out one-arm hug.

"I've been waiting all month for thith hug," Robb moaned.

"I bet you have!" Maddie replied, pulling away efficiently.

"... since the divorce, it's juth been ..." Robb continued.

Maddie shooed the diminutive dweeb toward the open bar and turned her attention to the next group filing into the gala. Her nonprofit agency's annual marquee event had sold out to capacity of 200 guests and as the fundraising director, she still had checks to collect at the door.

Robb posted up at the cocktail bar. When it came to getting Maddie's attention, he could wait. He always did.

When Maddie organized her sorority's year-long philanthropy campaign, she never expected the project would lead to a post-college job offer and lucrative career in fundraising. Five years after graduation, Maddie was now one of the highest paid employees of the regional nonprofit, and for good reason - she had expanded the group's efforts beyond its old generic campaigns and incorporated sophisticated data mining and social media appeals.

None of that mattered to Robb. He cared less about Maddie's legwork and more about her legs, less about her data sets and more about *dat ass*. He was constantly screening local nonprofit networks for young women who might be impressed by his ties to the business community and his nice-guy offers to help advance careers. As a former city official, Robb's nonprofit relied on a nebulous web of government grants. Greasy "networking" was his natural approach.

Over the years, Maddie stiff-armed Robb's incessant questions about her dating life. She used single and divorced female acquaintances as shiny objects to divert his attention, which she expected to be a successful gambit ever since Robb's divorce. She invented phantom boyfriends and even mentioned real anecdotes about men in her life to dissuade his interrogations. It was mostly futile.

"You going home with your banker boyfriend tonight?" Robb texted later during the dinner program, referring to a random donor Maddie chatted with briefly at the sign-in table. Robb was always watching, especially when she was talking to a man. Maddie looked over at Robb's table and was met with a googly-eyed glare. She forced a half-smile.

"He's gonna miss out on this view!" Robb texted immediately, attaching a creepshot of Maddie he had taken during the cocktail hour.

Maddie turned away immediately, before Robb could see her face get flushed with embarrassment and muted anger. Only real men get to see my body flushed, she reminded herself. And the big-bucks beta boy didn't qualify.

Maddie stepped into the hallway and thumbed through the stack of donor checks. Robb had committed to buying three tables but wrote his group's check to cover the price of five.

Maddie was used to Robb's grand gestures, but this was *way* over the top – even for a guy who made his career spending other people's money. Despite the challenging economic environment, tonight's event set a record for fundraising – and it wouldn't have been possible without Robb.

The rush and relief of the giant haul made it easier for Maddie to dissociate from Robb's generalized ick. She reminded herself that Robb was like a human ATM – if the bank machines had little man syndrome and slithered past women by grabbing their hips.

Maddie strode back into the room and noticed Robb pointing his phone in her direction to take another creepshot. *I guess every ATM has a camera*, she laughed to herself.

Individual/book club discussion

1.) Maddie's nonprofit has a sexual harassment policy designed to protect employees. Do you expect she'll report Robb?
2.) Would *you* report Robb?
3.) As Robb ratches up his spigot of charity campaign contributions, how might you anticipate his actions to evolve or devolve?

Gratitude

Thanks to the women of the LLC for their individual and collective experiences that inspired the Male Admirer Matrix.

Thanks to the three authors heavily cited in this book – Rollo Tomassi, Rian Stone and Richard Cooper – for their massive body of life-changing work. As the cliché goes, they walked so the rest of us could run – or as Cooper might say, they established fertile fields so Steve from Accounting could plow.

Though not cited in text, thanks to Coach Greg Adams for more than a decade of content on the psychology of simps (and the value of junior colleges.) You can find him on Instagram at @CoachGregAdamsTV.

Thanks to Ryan Holiday, whose *Ego is the Enemy* and *The Obstacle is the Way* helped me view my ego as a daily sparring partner.

Thanks to my morning radio co-host Brad Hildebrand – the owner of 104.5 FM (KSLQ) in St. Louis – whose verbal jousting has made me incrementally more tolerant and empathetic to Boomers' blue-pill operant conditioning.

And thanks to **you** for purchasing and reading this book. If you found it to be an enjoyable experience, I'd appreciate if you give it a 5-star review on Amazon.

About the author

John Combest co-hosts The Brad & John Show with Brad Hildebrand on 104.5 FM (KSLQ) in St. Louis, Missouri. After 12 ½ years in corporate communications at a Fortune 500 company, John wrote *Stalking, Harassment, Internet Trolling: A Guide to Recovering and Rebuilding After Online Attacks* in 2022. You can find excerpts of his books – and clips from The Brad & John Show – at johncombestblog.com.

Contact John here:

P.O. Box 512

Chesterfield, MO 63006

E-mail: john@johncombestblog.com

Instagram: @johncombest

facebook.com/johncombestauthor

www.ingramcontent.com/pod-product-compliance
Lightning Source LLC
Chambersburg PA
CBHW071411040426
42444CB00009B/2200